Corporate Sustainability

Corporate Sustainability

Shareholder Primacy Versus Stakeholder Primacy

Zabihollah Rezaee

Leader in applied, concise business books

Corporate Sustainability: Shareholder Primacy Versus Stakeholder Primacy

Copyright © Business Expert Press, LLC, 2021.

Cover design by Charlene Kronstedt

Interior design by Exeter Premedia Services Private Ltd., Chennai, India

First published in 2021 by
Business Expert Press, LLC
222 East 46th Street, New York, NY 10017
www.businessexpertpress.com

ISBN-13: 978-1-63742-086-7 (paperback)
ISBN-13: 978-1-63742-087-4 (e-book)

Business Expert Press Corporate Governance Collection

Collection ISSN: 1948-0470 (print)
Collection ISSN: 1948-0415 (electronic)

First edition: 2021

10 9 8 7 6 5 4 3 2 1

Description

Corporate sustainability has become an economic, moral, and strategic imperative with the potential to create shared value for all stakeholders. Public companies in the United States have traditionally operated under the corporate model of "shareholder primacy" that makes the board of directors' judiciary responsible only to shareholders in protecting their interests. Under the shareholder primacy system, the primary purpose of a corporation is to generate returns for shareholders, and thus corporate activities are managed toward creating shareholder value. This shareholder primacy system is also known as U.S. corporate governance model and is being criticized for focusing on generating short-term profits for shareholders while compromising long-term sustainability performance that creates shared value for all stakeholders and promotes innovation, growth, and the social and environmental impacts. The stakeholder primacy system, which is better known as the European corporate governance model, makes the board of directors' fiduciary responsible to protecting interests of all stakeholders including shareholders, creditors, employees, customers, suppliers, society, and the environment.

Recently, the Business Roundtable (BRT) announced the adoption of a new Statement on the Purpose of a Corporation, signed by 181 high-powered chief executive officers (CEOs), which recommend the move away from the shareholder primacy concept toward the stakeholder primacy concept that promotes sustainability of creating shared value for all stakeholders. Corporate purpose and stakeholder considerations have gained recognition in the business community worldwide. The stakeholder primacy challenges companies to put stakeholders at the heart of a company's purpose. A shift in corporate purpose from shareholder primacy to stakeholder primacy, reinforced by the U.S. BRT's Statement on the Purpose of a Corporation. This focus, combined with public pressure for CEOs to engage on social and political topics, and human capital (HC) (e.g., HC, diversity, immigration, gun control, and gender pay equity), enables corporate America to advance toward business sustainability.

The board's role under stakeholder primacy/capitalism as opposed to shareholder primacy/capitalism is to oversee the managerial function of focusing on the long-term sustainability performance, effectively communicating sustainability performance information to all stakeholders. The board should be informed and understand the stakeholder objectives; rationales for focusing on sustainability factors of performance; risk and disclosure; and managerial strategic planning, sustainable operational performance, and executive compensation in promoting long-term corporate value. The board should also provide oversight, insight, and foresight function on the achievement of both financial economic sustainability performance (ESP) and nonfinancial environmental, social, governance, and ethical (ESGE) sustainability performance driven from financial, human, social, environmental, and manufacturing capitals, as well as innovation, culture, and corporate governance.

Specifically,

1. Present shareholder primacy and stakeholder primacy concepts.
2. Discuss all five dimensions of sustainability performance including economic, governance, social, ethical, and environmental (EGSEE) with a keen focus on economic sustainability performance.
3. Examine all corporate capitals including reputational, financial, manufacturing, environmental, human, and social.
4. Address directors' and executives' roles and responsibilities under shareholder primacy and stakeholder primacy concepts.

Keywords

corporate sustainability; financial economic sustainability performance; nonfinancial environmental, ethical, social, and governance sustainability performance; sustainability risk; sustainability disclosure; stakeholder primacy; shareholder primacy; shareholder capitalism; stakeholder capitalism; sustainability capitals; sustainability standard-setting organizations

Contents

Preface

Business sustainability has gained considerable attention from investors, regulators, standard-setters, business organization, academics, and the accounting profession in recent decades. This book defines business sustainability as a process of generating financial economic sustainability performance to create shareholder value, while achieving nonfinancial environmental, ethical, social, and governance sustainability performance in protecting the interests of other stakeholders including creditors, customers, employees, suppliers, government, society, and the environment. The role of business corporations in our society has evolved from profit maximization to creating shareholder value and, in recent years, to create shared value for all stakeholders. This book offers guidance to organizations for choosing between shareholder primacy and stakeholder primacy, and thus presents corporate governance in the context of shareholder capitalism model and stakeholder capitalism model. This book provides insights into managerial initiatives for advancing enterprise sustainability from greenwashing and business branding to creating opportunities for revenue generation, cost management, supply chain, business growth, and product and service innovation.

This book consists of four chapters covering all aspects of corporate sustainability with a keen focus on sustainability capitals, shareholder primacy, and stakeholder primacy concepts. Anyone who is involved with business sustainability and corporate governance, the financial reporting process, investment decisions, legal and financial advising, audit functions, and corporate governance education will be interested in this book. Specifically, corporations, their executives, the boards of directors, board committees, internal and external auditors, accountants, lawmakers, regulators, standard-setters, users of financial statements (investors, creditors, and pensioners), investor activists, business schools, and other professionals (attorneys, financial analysts, and bankers) will benefit from this book.

The primary theme of this book is on the examination of stakeholder primacy/capitalism and shareholder primacy/capitalism. As the book was going through the production and publication process, the International Business Council (IBC) of the World Economic Forum (WEF), in collaboration with the big 4 accounting firms, has released its final recommendations for a set of globally accepted, standardized, and industry-oriented environmental, social, and governance (ESG) sustainability performance metrics and disclosures. These recommendations suggest a move away from shareholder primacy and capitalism toward stakeholder primacy and capitalism. These recommendations are intended to provide guiding principles for focusing on the ESG sustainability factors of performance, risk, and disclosures on governance, people, planet, and prosperity. This book also highlights how people, business, and resources collaborate in a business sustainability and accountability model. This book is intended to cover a variety of issues relevant to business sustainability and their implications for organizations of all types and sizes. I hope you find this book relevant and useful to gain and maintain your business and personal sustainability.

Sincerely,

Zabihollah (Zabi) Rezaee

February 16, 2021

Acknowledgments

I acknowledge the Securities and Exchange Commission, the Public Company Accounting Oversight Board, the American Institute of Certified Public Accountants, the Big Four Accounting Firms and Corporate Governance Organizations, American Accounting Association, Global Reporting Initiative (GRI), International Integrated Reporting Council (IIRC), Sustainability Accounting Standards Board (SASB), United Nations, International Business Council (IBC) of the World Economic Forum (WEF), and other sustainability standard-setting organizations for permission to quote and reference their professional standards and other publications.

The encouragement and support of my colleagues at the University of Memphis are also acknowledged, especially my graduate assistants Ms. Naomi Riley and Vy Nguyen for providing invaluable assistance. I thank the members of the Business Expert Press team and Exeter team for their hard work and dedication in editing the book, including Scott Isenberg and John Wood.

My sincere thanks are due to my wife Soheila and my children Rose and Nick. Without their love, enthusiasm, and support, this book would not have come to fruition when it did.

Zabihollah (Zabi) Rezaee
February 16, 2021

CHAPTER 1

Introduction to Shareholder Capitalism and Stakeholder Capitalism

Executive Summary

Corporate sustainability has become an economic and strategic imperative with the potential to create shared value for all stakeholders. Public companies in the United States have traditionally operated under the corporate model of "shareholder primacy/capitalism" that makes the board of directors' fiduciary responsible primarily to shareholders with protected interests. Under the shareholder primacy system, the primary purpose of a corporation is to generate returns for shareholders, and thus corporate activities are managed toward creating shareholder value. The stakeholder primacy/capitalism, which is better known as the European corporate governance model, makes the board of directors' fiduciary responsible of protecting interests for all stakeholders including shareholders, creditors, employees, customers, suppliers, society, and the environment. The 2020 COVID-19 pandemic has been an exogenous shock in the global economy and capital market with substantial impacts on individuals, organizations, and society. The pandemic also demands that business organizations focus on safety, health, and well-being of their employees, customers, and suppliers, and thus a global move toward stakeholder primacy. This introductory chapter describes the models of shareholder primacy and stakeholder primacy, and the next three chapters provide more in-depth discussion of these models.

Introduction

Shareholder primacy is a concept that makes the board of directors' fiduciary responsible only to shareholders in protecting their interests with the main mission of creating value primarily for the shareholders. This shareholder primacy system is also known as U.S. corporate governance model and is being criticized for focusing on generating short-term profits for shareholders while compromising long-term sustainability performance that creates shared value for all stakeholders and promotes innovation, growth, and social and environmental impacts. Corporations can create the right balance between the wealth maximization for shareholders under the shareholder primacy concept, while achieving the welfare maximization for all stakeholders under the stakeholder primacy concept.

Recently, the Business Roundtable (BRT) announced the adoption of a new Statement on the Purpose of a Corporation, signed by 181 high-powered chief executive officers (CEOs), which recommend the move away from the shareholder primacy concept toward the stakeholder primacy concept that promotes sustainability of creating shared value for all stakeholders.[1] Corporate purpose and stakeholder considerations have gained recognition in the business community worldwide. The stakeholder primacy challenges companies to put stakeholders at the heart of a company's purpose. A shift in corporate purpose from shareholder primacy to stakeholder primacy reinforced by the U.S. BRT's Statement on the Purpose of a Corporation. This focus, combined with public pressure for CEOs to engage on social and political topics (e.g., human capital, diversity, immigration, gun control, and gender pay equity), enables corporate America to advance toward business sustainability. This chapter provides a synopsis of shareholder primacy and stakeholder primacy models.

Book Objectives and Sustainability Definition

The primary objective of this book is to focus on shareholder primacy and stakeholder primacy models of business sustainability by contrasting and comparing these models and their relevance in advancing business sustainability. Business sustainability is defined as a process of achieving financial economic sustainability performance (ESP) to create shareholder value while generating nonfinancial environmental, ethical, social, and governance (EESG) sustainability performance in protecting the interest of other stakeholders. Stakeholders are those who have stake in the organization and take risk and share returns including shareholders, employees, creditors, customers, suppliers, society, and the environment.

Business sustainability can best be promoted under the stakeholder primacy model. The board's role under stakeholder primacy/capitalism as opposed to shareholder primacy/capitalism is to oversee the managerial function of focusing on the long-term sustainability performance, effectively communicating sustainability performance information to all stakeholders. The board should be informed and able to comprehend the stakeholder objectives, rationales for focusing on sustainability factors of performance, risk, and disclosure, and managerial strategic planning, sustainable operational performance, and executive compensation in promoting long-term corporate value. The board should also provide oversight, insight, and foresight function on the achievement of both financial ESP and nonfinancial EESG sustainability performance driven from financial, human, social, environmental, and manufacturing capitals as well as innovation, culture, and corporate governance. The concept of impact investing (II) in achieving desired financial returns for investors while generating social and environmental impacts is relevant and important under the stakeholder primacy model.

Recently, a definition of corporate purpose has been proposed and elaborated to include three key guiding principles as follows:[2]

1. The proposed definition of corporate purpose for publicly traded business (for-profit) corporations is to measure their actions by what is in the best interests of *shareholders* (the shareholder primacy governance model).
2. In reaching for this new corporate purpose definition, the reality is ignored that the shareholder primacy governance model embraces the ability of directors to consider a broad array of nonfinancial EESG sustainability performance factors.
3. Companies who chose to address EESG/stakeholder-oriented decisions pursuant to the stakeholder interests balancing act

contemplated by the proposed new purpose definition run the risk of losing the valuable protection of the business judgment rule.

The COVID-19 pandemic has brought on many challenges, including focusing on the inequality in our society and the fact that many public companies' primary goal is maximizing shareholder value at the expense of other stakeholders such as employees, creditors, customers, suppliers, and communities. However, under their new corporate purpose definition, directors will have "latitude to make decisions that reasonably balance the interests of all constituencies" and they urge corporations and their shareholders to "recognize that ESG and stakeholder purpose are necessary elements of sustainable business success."[3] Thus, public companies should ensure that they have effective corporate governance structure and measures to creating shared value for all stakeholders and serving the interests of all stakeholders including shareholders. Public companies and their elected board of directors and appointed management should be responsible and accountable to shareholders and ensure that they run the company in the best interests of shareholders in creating sustainable and long-term value.

Impact Investing

The relationship between financial/market performance and nonfinancial EESG performance has been extensively yet inconclusively debated in the literature in the past decade, which suggests that investors pay attention to sustainability factors of risk, performance, and disclosure. A growing number of investors are now considering II with a keen focus on financial return and EESG sustainability factors and integrating nonfinancial EESG sustainability factors into their investment strategies.[4] The Global Impact Investing Network (GIIN) refers to II as "investments made with the intention to generate a positive, measurable, social, and environmental impact alongside a financial return."[5] Regulators have responded to the demand for environmental, social, and governance (ESG) information and have either mandated ESG sustainability performance disclosure (European Union, EU Directive, 2014) as more than 6,000 European public companies are required to disclose their ESG information in the fiscal 2017 year and onward or recommended voluntary disclosure of ESG information.[6]

Corporate purpose and stakeholder considerations have gained recognition in the business community worldwide. In August 2019, 181 out of 188 member CEOs of the U.S. BRT signed an amended Statement on the Purpose of a Corporation, moving away from the traditional shareholder primacy of maximizing shareholder returns.[7] The stakeholder primacy challenges companies to put stakeholders at the heart of a company's purpose. A shift in corporate purpose from shareholder primacy to stakeholder primacy reinforced by the U.S. BRT's Statement on the Purpose of a Corporation. The idea of establishing the purpose for the company beyond profit maximization for shareholders, combined with public pressure from investors and regulators to engage on social and political topics (e.g., human capital, diversity, immigration, gun control, and gender pay equity) has encouraged business organizations to define their purpose and focus on II. The concept of II suggests that corporations achieve a desired rate of returns for their shareholders while generating social and environmental impacts. Although the II concept has often been used interchangeably with socially responsible investing (SRI), the two concepts have important differences. SRI is commonly referred to as the investment strategy that maximizes financial returns while minimizing any negative impact on the society or environment, whereas II is a deliberate investment strategy to achieve both financial returns and social and/or environmental impacts.[8]

The distinction between II and SRI investment strategies is important for several reasons. First, investor sentiment plays a role in firms' commitment to II when investors place a valuation premium on nonfinancial EESG sustainability performance. Second, in the aftermath of the COVID-19 pandemic considering financial and operational challenges, firms, their shareholders, and directors have increasingly become attuned to EESG considerations in allocating scares resources between II and SRI investments in achieving EESG objectives. Third, investors now pay more attention to EESG initiatives and investments as asset managers of the Big 3 investment families (BlackRock, State Street, and Vanguard) consider EESG risks and opportunities in their investment strategies.[9] Finally, investors with stronger EESG preferences with a focus on II with portfolios that tilt more toward green assets earn lower expected returns than investors with a focus on SRI investing in brown assets.

Defining corporate purpose has been a key trend in Europe over the last several years and will continue to spread in 2020. In France, expect more companies to adopt a "raison d'être" (corporate purpose), an expectation which may become a legal requirement. The raison d'être gives a sense of meaning to stakeholders and puts EESG at the core of corporate strategy. Climate change and transitioning to a lower-carbon economy are also top priorities for European stakeholders. Boards will need to be able to understand and discuss ESG data—and its impact on key matters such as executive remuneration—with investors. In France, the number of board committees focused on ESG has doubled in the last two years. This is an important development, as EESG is the focus of a quarter of the questions raised at general assemblies and half the resolutions submitted by shareholders. In Spain, investors will begin to exercise their vote on nonfinancial reporting. Spain also is extending its corporate governance principles, which promote key components of EESG, to private companies in 2020. More transparent sustainability disclosures on long-term economic and EESG performance create opportunities to identify and correct operational inefficiencies, reputational and financial risks that would improve economic performance and thus increase the firm value.[10]

Investors typically have incomplete financial and nonfinancial information about a firm's ESG sustainability performance and thus they may not be aware of the firm's governance effectiveness, ethical culture, and social and environmental commitments. Lack of knowledge on the part of investors reduces the firm's investor base, which in turn makes risk sharing incomplete and inefficient and thus stocks of these firms are out of line with their market's fundamentals, which may incentivize firms to obtain certification to influence stock prices. Disclosures of sustainability information however make investors aware of the firm existence and enlarge its investor base, which improves risk sharing and thus make their stocks closer to their market fundamentals. Stakeholders may attempt to pressure and/or motivate firms to disclose sustainability information about their social, governance, and environmental activities and release of such information leads to disclosure of private information. Managers tend to analyze the costs/benefits of obtaining sustainability ranking to improve sustainability disclosures and how these disclosures are integrated and observed by capital markets.

Sustainability information on long-term economic and EESG performance increases the quality and quantity of the firm's disclosures, and thus more focus on long-term and sustainable performance and fewer incentives for short-term performance that could be detrimental to the long-term sustainability. Given that sustainability disclosing firms provide fewer incentives and opportunities for short-termism, we expect to find a positive relation between sustainability disclosure and its rankings and stock prices.

Investor interest in sustainable investments, products, and services has increased, and policy makers have begun to take a greater focus on this area along with a broad set of stakeholders as well. The demand for sustainability policies and initiatives is growing in velocity and required by some nations. However, other topics must be addressed before discussing the sustainability policies that should be implemented into the business environment. First, a well-regulated sustainable finance ecosystem is needed to support broader sustainability-related policy initiatives at the global level, most pointedly to mobilize the massive amount of capital needed to address climate change. Second, and by no means unrelated, is the concern that robust standards exist to mitigate the risk of "greenwashing"—the risk that either through confusing or outright misleading investment approaches, asset owners cannot make informed choices about the actual sustainability characteristics of their investments.[11] The push for sustainability has reached global standards and already proven to be a colossal game changer that even alters the behavior of both institutional investors and companies in various diverse ways. While investors struggle with the challenge of integrating EESG factors into their investment decisions, many companies want to define a meaningful corporate purpose to exploit the full potential of sustainability reporting. These goals can be achieved by the following:[12]

- Doing a more effective job managing relations with institutional investors and shareholders.
- Reshaping corporate reporting to provide a holistic picture of the business and its value drivers.

- Directing shareholders' attention to the company's unique characteristics and values.
- Designating company-specific performance metrics linked to business strategy and value creation.
- Reducing investors' reliance on external one-size-fits-all standards and inappropriate metrics.
- Reducing vulnerability to shareholder activism.

Some estimate that the amount of money being committed to impact the investing strategies used around the world has grown to $502 billion, according to the analysis by the GIIN. In a white paper published in April 2019, the GIIN estimated that over 800 asset managers now account for about 50 percent of assets focused on II, while 31 development finance institutions manage just over a quarter of industry assets and several large investment firms manage over $1 billion each.[13] The Big 3 asset management firms of BlackRock, Vanguard, and State Street have responsibility to manage, monitor, and disclose their role as stewards of their clients' investment by engaging with public companies' board of directors and management on material business issues including financial returns on investment and nonfinancial EESG sustainability factors of performance, risk, and disclosure.

Shareholder Primacy and Capitalism Model

Public companies in the United States have traditionally operated under the corporate model of "shareholder primacy" and "shareholder capitalism," which suggests the primary goal of business organizations is to maximize profit and thus wealth for shareholders. This model makes the board of directors' fiduciary responsible primarily to shareholders in protecting their interests. Under the shareholder primacy system, the primary purpose of a corporation is to generate returns for shareholders, and thus corporate activities are managed toward creating shareholder value. This shareholder primacy system is also known as U.S. corporate governance model and is being criticized for focusing on generating short-term profits for shareholders, while compromising long-term sustainability performance that creates shared value for all stakeholders and promotes innovation, growth, and the social and environmental impacts. Shareholders have the right to vote to nominate, elect, remove the board of directors, approve executive compensation, mandate the corporate charter and bylaws, approve the appointment of auditors, and approve major transactions including mergers and acquisitions. In general, shareholders are enabled to vote on business matters that are relevant to the protection of their investment including the right to full, fair, and timely information following the guiding principle of "one share, one vote."

The U.S. capital markets driven by the shareholder primacy and capitalism model have been perceived as promoting shareholder wealth maximization without creating an inclusive and equitable economy for all Americans. However, in recent years, some progresses have been made to promote capital stewardship to preserve market mechanisms in creating shared value for all stakeholders in a more equitable economic system. The prevailing laws, regulations, and culture governing U.S. capital markets are intended to maximize profit for companies and their shareholders, regardless of the damage caused by just focusing on maximizing profit such as negative impacts on society and the environment. This shareholder primacy and shareholder capitalism model should be modified and reformed to promote business sustainability.

Bridgewater Associate, Ray Dalio, states that capitalism is a fundamentally sound system, but that it is not working well for the majority of people in the current times; therefore, it requires revision to provide more equal opportunities. To make the changes, Dalio believes the following is needed:[14]

1. Leadership from the top.
2. Bipartisan and skilled shapers of policy working together to redesign the system, so it works better.
3. Clear metrics that can be used to judge success and hold the people in charge accountable for achieving it.
4. Redistribution of resources that will improve both the well-being and productivities of the vast majority of people by:
   (a) Creating private–public partnerships that would jointly vet and invest in double bottom line projects that would be judged on the basis of their social and economic performance results relative to clear metrics.

(b) Raising money in ways that both improve conditions and improve the economy's productivity by taking into consideration the all-in costs for the society.

(c) Raising more from the top via taxes that would be engineered to not have disruptive effects on productivity and that would be earmarked to help those in the middle and the bottom, primarily in ways that also improve the economy's overall level of productivity, so that the spending on these programs is largely paid for by the cost savings and income improvements that they create.

5. Coordination of monetary and fiscal policies.[15]

Many corporate leaders have stronger incentives to give substantial weight to the interests of stakeholders because it betters their own interests, but there is no incentive to advance their interests beyond that to what would benefit the shareholder. An empirical analysis of over 100 private equity acquisitions governed by constituency statutes provides novel evidence that supports clear verdict on the success of these statutes.[16] The advocates of adopting these statutes touted their promise for addressing concerns related to stakeholders, and this promise enabled corporate leaders to obtain the support of labor and other stakeholder groups for the legislation.

The voluntary nature of EESG disclosure under the shareholder primacy system enables managers to exercise judgment in deciding the level of EESG sustainability focus and presenting the type and extent of EESG disclosure. Whether managers exercise such discretion in an efficient manner consistent with long-term sustainable returns and EESG principles to create shared value for all stakeholders or in an opportunistic manner to enhance their reputation and generate near-term returns just for shareholders is debatable. Increased EESG sustainability disclosure can enable stakeholders (e.g., institutional investors, analysts, creditors, government, suppliers, society, and employees) to develop their own independent and informed views on firms' sustainable performance in all areas of economic, environmental, social, ethical, and governance activities. The recent 2020 KPMG survey focuses on the disclosure of these sustainability activities including reporting on climate-related risk and carbon reduction, United Nations Sustainable Development Goals

(SDGs) relevant to societal, environmental, and governance impacts, and the risk of biodiversity loss.[17]

Stakeholder Primacy and Stakeholder Capitalism Model

The stakeholder primacy system, which is better known as the European corporate governance model, makes the board of directors' fiduciary responsible for protecting the interests of all stakeholders, including shareholders, creditors, employees, customers, suppliers, society, and the environment. In this era of sustainability-oriented investors, directors, and executives' commitments to sustainability, a major challenge is determining the determinants and consequences of business sustainability. The major determinants of business sustainability are determined by the shareholder primacy and stakeholder primacy system and other considerations including the firm's size, leveraged, maturity, complexity, merger and acquisition activity, restructuring charges, and operate in a more litigious industry, corporate governance measures, and internal control effectiveness. Business sustainability consequences are the three sustainability factors of performance, disclosure, and risk, as well as financial and market performance, earnings quality, and financial reporting conservatism. The stakeholder capitalism model focuses on the II concept of generating desired financial returns on investments by shareholder, while protecting interests of other stakeholders and achieving social and environmental impacts. Under the stakeholder primacy model, while shareholders have the right to protect their investments, they also benefit in the long term where their company is sustainable in creating shared value for all stakeholders. Shareholder welfare creation, rather than shareholder wealth creation, is promoted under the stakeholder capitalism.

Shareholder Capitalism Versus Stakeholder Capitalism

The concept of shareholder primacy where public companies are managed solely in protecting the interests of the shareholders has been debated. There has been a move toward the adoption of the stakeholder primacy concept where business organizations are run in the interests of all stakeholders including shareholders. In the Summer of 2019, the BRT released an updated purpose of corporation statement that disavows the endorsement of shareholder primacy, suggesting that the corporations should not solely serve its shareholders, but rather all stakeholders. This statement was signed by 181 CEOs of large companies such as Apple and JPMorgan. Much has been written about this statement and its effects on the economy and specifically the shareholders. In one article, the authors state that this transition will cause our economy to suffer due to company cash becoming trapped inside public firms, poorly invested resources, and as shareholder payouts decline the smaller firms will have even less access to capital.[18] The vitality of our economy very well depends on shareholder interests; however, stakeholder interest must now be addressed as well.

In "The Illusory Promise of Stakeholder Governance," Lucian Bebchuk and Roberto Tallarita reject the idea of stakeholderism stating that it does not benefit stakeholders, shareholders, or society.[19] Bebchuk and Tallarita believe that directors of a company are not motivated enough or even able to promote anything other than shareholder value in this system focused on shareholder profit. Contradiction of this research comes from Colin Mayer who commented on the possibility of a misconceived contradiction of shareholderism versus stakeholderism, by arguing that stakeholder governance is either enlightened shareholder value and nothing more, or that it imposes unmanageable trade-offs on company directors.[20] Mayer instead suggests that instead of describing the system as it is known today, we should analyze what it could or should be to provide a more accurate benchmark against which it would be possible to evaluate the stakeholder versus shareholder system.

Several initiatives are taken to move away from the shareholder primacy and toward stakeholder primacy under the new corporate governance model including the following:

1. The board fiduciary duty should be extended to all stakeholders and the board of directors should be accountable to all stakeholders not just shareowners.
2. Corporate purpose statements should specifically state that corporations positively benefit society in the context of creating shared value for all stakeholders.

3. Multiple stakeholders including employees should be represented on corporate boards.

4. Large corporations should be required to charter federally, to enable the accountable governance reforms that require responsibility to all stakeholders.

5. ESG Disclosure Simplification Act (link between ESP and ESG).

6. The Shareholder Protection Act (political spending).

7. Corporate Human Rights Risk Assessment, Prevention, and Mitigation Act of 2019 (human rights risks or impacts on the operations).

8. Climate Risk Disclosure Act of 2019 (financial and business risks associated with climate change).

9. Accountable Capitalism Act of 2018 (Senator Warren, Corporations with revenue over $1 billion would be required to obtain a federal *corporate charter*, two-fifth of the directors shall be elected by employees, and any political spending over $10,000 has approval of both 75 percent of shareholders).

Conclusion

In a time of high uncertainty, anxiety, complexity, and ambiguity triggered by the 2020 COVID-19 pandemic, business organizations are better off by focusing on the stakeholder primacy concept of creating shared value for all stakeholders. Thus, sustainability strategies have become integral components of business environment and corporate culture. This emerging trend of moving away from shareholder primacy toward stakeholder primacy and index funding has led to a debate centered on the implications of common ownership and main mission of business organizations.

Under the stakeholder primacy model, there is a spread ownership, and the main mission is to create shared value for all stakeholders. Policy makers, regulators, and society have questioned on the fiduciary model of shareholder primacy and advocates moving toward stakeholder primacy. The shareholder primacy model has served investors well in creating value and maximizing wealth for them, but is being criticized for focusing on serving only one group of stakeholders and generating short-term profits at the expense of long-term sustainability performance, innovation, and growth. This model often ignores the social and environmental impacts of corporations. The focus on shareholder wealth creation may not benefit other stakeholders, such as employees, customers, creditors, suppliers, government, society, and the environment. Business organizations are given rights to operate and generate profits for their shareholders, but with these rights come public interests and societal responsibilities of having social and environmental impacts.

Chapter Takeaways

- Promote profit-with-purpose mission to create shared value for all stakeholders.
- Consider moving away from the shareholder primacy model and moving toward the stakeholder primacy model.
- Achieve II purpose of generating desired financial returns for shareholders while achieving social and environmental impacts.
- Establish measures of both financial ESP performance and nonfinancial EESG sustainability performance.
- Communicate the achievement of both financial ESP performance and nonfinancial EESG sustainability performance to all stakeholders.

CHAPTER 2

Corporate Capitals

Executive Summary

Business sustainability can be beneficial to both internal and external stakeholders. Stakeholders are those who have vested interests in a firm through their investments in the form of financial capital (shareholders), human capital (HC) (employees), physical capital (customers and suppliers), social capital (society), environmental capital (the environment), and regulatory capital (government). This chapter presents all types of capitals and their integrated contribution to and effects on business sustainability.

Introduction

Traditionally, business organizations have focused on the role of financial capital in creating value for shareholders. Recent move toward and acceptance of business sustainability encourages business organization to pay attention to other capitals in creating shared value for all stakeholders. The magnitude of environmental, ethical, social, governance (EESG) sustainability-focused investment is now more than $20 trillion. EESG funds require that corporations define their purpose of generating financial returns and achieving social and environmental impacts. For many years, the focus on profit maximization for shareholders worked in U.S. financial markets. Globalization and technological advances, and often disruption, have forced corporations to focus on the short-termism of meeting or beating analysts' forecast expectations. However, corporations are now facing pressures from social activists and stakeholders to pay attention to the interests of customers, suppliers, employees, society, and the environment, among others, to create shared value for all stakeholders. Achievement of financial economic sustainability performance

(ESP) and nonfinancial EESG sustainability performance requires business organizations and their board of directors and executives effectively utilize financial and nonfinancial capitals presented in this chapter.

Types of Capitals

Business organizations have traditionally employed financial capital, both equity and debt capitals, in financing and acquiring assets to use in the operation in generating revenues with less focus on nonfinancial capitals. The recent move toward sustainability requires business organizations to utilize all types of financial capital (equity and debt) and nonfinancial capital (strategic, reputational, human, social, and environmental) to generate shared value for all stakeholders. Figure 2.1 presents sustainability capital stewardship and all associated capitals including strategic, operational, financial, human, social, environmental, reputational/trust, and intellectual. The Committee of Sponsoring Organizations of the Treadway Commission (COSO) and the World Business Council for Sustainable Development (WBCSD) issued "Guidance for Applying Enterprise Risk Management (ERM) to Environmental, Social and Governance (ESG)-related Risks" in October 2018.[1] The COSO/WBCSD is intended to assist entities of all types and sizes to manage their sustainability ESG-related risks that affect their bottom-line financial earnings as well as business success and survival.

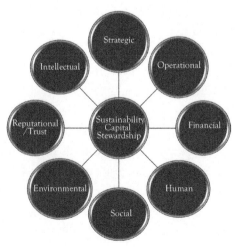

Figure 2.1 Sustainability capitals

There is no universal or agreed-upon definition of EESG-related risks also known as sustainability risk factors that may include the EESG-related risks and/or opportunities. Environmental risks are risks related to climate change, global warming natural resources, pollution, and waste and environmental opportunities. Ethical risks are failure of conducting business, ethically and legally in compliance with all applicable laws, rules, regulations, and standards. Social risks are risks related to HC, workplace conditions, product liability, stakeholder opposition, and social opportunities. Governance risks are risks related to corporate governance measures, noncompliance with all applicable laws and regulations, HC, product liability, stakeholder opposition, and social opportunity.

According to Paul Druckman, IIRC Chief Executive, there are over 1,000 businesses worldwide using Integrated Reporting in 27 countries.[2] The IIRC suggests six capitals as follows: (1) financial capital, (2) manufactured capital, (3) intellectual capital, (4) HC, (5) social and relationship capital, and (6) natural capital, which organizations can utilize in creating shared value for all stakeholders.[3] Management acts as the steward of strategic capital, financial capital, HC, social capital, and environmental capital, and acts as the active and long-term-oriented steward of all stakeholders including shareholders. Figure 2.1 shows eight sustainability capitals of strategic, financial, human, social, environmental, reputational/trust, intellectual, and manufactured. Some of these capitals are interrelated but they all collectively contribute to the creation of shared value for all stakeholders.

The ongoing challenges brought on by the COVID-19 pandemic while requiring management to simultaneously consider divergent economic, governance, social, and environmental issues enable management to effectively exercise stewardship over a broader range of business capital from financial capital to environmental, social, and reputational capital to ensure continuity and nonfinancial HC of protecting safety, health, and well-being of employees, customers, and suppliers. The relationship between business, society, and the environment is complex and often tense and becomes more relevant in the post-COVID-19 era because management is now required to be a good steward of all capitals from financial to human, environmental, and social.

Strategic Capital

Strategic capital relates to management strategic planning and being accountable for strategic plans, decisions, and actions. Strategic planning is a process of establishing purpose and mission, making decisions, taking actions documenting and communicating plans of actions throughout the organization to those who are affected by actions, evaluating compliance with actions, and holding individuals accountable. The strategic plans enable organizations to document their purpose, mission, values and vision, and values as well as establishing goals and the action plans to implement them. The economic order, stakeholder expectations, corporate culture, and business environment are changing in the post-COVID-19 era, and how business organizations define their purpose and measure the achievement of their success are changing too. Purpose determines why the organization exists, what is its mission, who are the stakeholders, and what are its objectives and strategies in achieving the objectives. The main objective function for any business organization has been and continues to be the creation of shared value for all stakeholders including shareholders, creditors, customers, suppliers, employees, government, society, and the environment. Changes in the purpose, mission, objectives, and strategies for business organization in the aftermath of the COVID-19 crisis are important to the long-term sustainability of the organization.

Every company should have its unique purpose determined in its charter of incorporation to maximize its positive impacts on all stakeholders including society and the environment and to minimize the negative impacts on multistakeholders. In case of nonexistence of and/or inadequate "Statement of Purpose," all executives in the c-suite under the oversight function of the board of directors and approval by majority shareholders should establish an appropriate stakeholder-inclusive "Statement of Purpose." The purpose of profit maximization and shareholder wealth creation has changed to create shared value for all stakeholders. To effectively achieve this new purpose, corporations are expanding their performance to both financial/quantitative economic performance (ESP) and nonfinancial/qualitative EESG sustainability performance. Sustainability has become an economic and strategic imperative with potential to create opportunities and risks for businesses.

Mission reflects the organization's determination to stay with its purpose and its achievement in the short-, medium-, and long term. Companies are now adopting the corporate mission of profit with purpose in creating shared value for all stakeholders by shifting their goals to create shareholder value while fulfilling their social, environmental, and governance responsibilities. Corporate objectives have sustainably changed in the post-COVID-19 pandemic to survival in the short term, continuity in the medium term, and sustainability in the long term. The board of directors pay more attention to the well-being, safety, and health of their employees, customers, and suppliers.

In the aftermath of recent financial crises, it is not uncommon for investors to lose confidence in firms. The board of directors can rebuild trust by starting off with focusing on more long-term goals. While the board has fiduciary duties to carry out, a lot of times they fall prey to pressures of obtaining immediate results, which may deviate from the long-term picture. Instead, strategies should be implemented that would allow the firm to withstand short-term pressures. The board's priorities should be more focused, which can be achieved by the board delegating duties to the committees that do not require the board's full attention, allowing the board to focus on the priorities of the company. In order to rebuild trust, directors must always act in the best interests of the company, even if it means disagreeing with shareholders and risking reelection. Strong communication with shareholders should be established in order to understand their concerns, ideas, feedback, and if there is any disconnection in their views. Strategic capital reflects the organization's value, vision, culture, purpose, mission, goals, objectives, plans of actions, and accountability.

Operational Capital

A firm's operational capital reflects an organization's resources in producing goods and services demanded by their constituencies and stakeholders that are not detrimental to society and the environment. Corporate culture of integrity and competency plays an important role in establishing policies, procedures, and processes to utilize maximization of the operational capital. The board of directors as representative of shareholders should design directions for operational efficiency and effectiveness and guide management to implement and maintain policies and procedures to achieve both financial ESP and nonfinancial EESG performance in creating shared value for all stakeholders including shareholders, creditors, employees, customers, suppliers, communities, society, and the environment. The board of directors should oversee that the organization is pursuing the goal of sustainability performance and compliance with all applicable laws, rules, regulations, standards, and best practices. While the board of directors should avoid micromanaging operation, it should provide strategic directions for management to continuously improve efficiency and effectiveness. Effective corporate governance measures should be placed to promote vigilant oversight function by the board of directors, effective managerial function by the management, and accountable and responsible actions by other corporate gatekeepers including auditors and financial advisors.

Financial Capital

Financial capital consists of both equity and debt capital. Financial ESP can be achieved by continuously improving capital productivity by optimizing supply chains, cost reengineering focused on reducing operating, production, and compliance costs, improving employee productivity and efficiency, and focusing on activities that create long-term, enduring, and sustainable financial performance. A focus on economic sustainability can also create opportunities for business innovation and growth by promoting sustainable products and services, new customer relationships, and new markets through environmentally friendly and socially acceptable products and services. ESP is measured in terms of long-term accounting-based measures (return on equity and sales), market-based measures (stock returns and market-book value), and long-term investments (R&D and advertising) and disclosed through a set of financial statements disseminated to shareholders in assessing the risk and return associated with their investments.

Human Capital

HC is an asset of skills processes by the labor force that can be utilized to generate other assets. HC is defined by the Organization for Economic

Co-operation and Development (OECD) as "the knowledge, skills, competencies and other attributes embodied in individuals or groups of individuals acquired during their life and used to produce goods, services or ideas in market circumstances."[4] HC is defined as attributes of labor that increase productivity and viewed as investment in labor including education, training, skills, capacity, health, ability to adapt to achieve productive capacity, goals, and maintain innovative and create economic value. HC factors as part of nonfinancial EESG sustainability are relevant and material to investors.

HC is becoming more important as a valuable and productive asset for public companies and employees are becoming important stakeholders for several reasons. First, employee participation in the production and service processes is essential as employee productivity improves corporate performance. Second, employees are becoming shareholders by investing in the company's shares through 401(K) and 529 plans and direct investment. Third, employees in many countries are given the opportunity to represent on the board of directors of public companies. Finally, the COVID-19 pandemic has caused business organizations to assess the HC risk by making safety, health, and well-being of employees, customers, and suppliers a prerequisite for reopening business. HC issues are relevant to the company's management of human resources as key assets to delivering long-term value. These issues that affect the company's bottom line through employee productivity, labor relations, and the health and safety of employees. HC is viewed as an important asset that contributes significantly to the long-term and sustainable value creation and value protection. There is a need for proper identification, measurement, recognition, and reporting HC.

One of the greatest concerns regarding HC is whether or how companies should get their stakeholders, especially their employees, involved in the process of making important corporate-level decisions, rather than pursuing the shareholder primacy model in which the benefits of shareholders are maximized. Some advantages of the shared governance (also known as codetermination) include better coordination, information flows between board and employees, employees' loyalty and motivation, implicit contracts enforcement, and alignment of shareholders and employees' interests. In the working paper "Labor in the Boardroom" in 2019, Jäger, Schoefer, and Heining exploit a 1994 reform experiment in

Germany, which mandated the representation of worker-elected directors in the board of some stock corporations, while eliminating board seats of workforce representatives in others. The result of the experiment shows that workers' participation in the board of directors actually increases capital by increasing production output per worker and reducing outsourcing. Despite no clear effect on financial capacity and profitability, shared governance is found to reduce interest payments over debt by an insignificant amount, and therefore, makes firms with worker-elected directors seem slightly less risky. It is also found that the lack of workforce representatives in the board tends to cause underinvestment, while codetermination can increase investment. However, too much worker bargaining power may result in some inefficiencies such as overinvestment. On top of that, if worker-elected directors only compose the minority of board seats, they tend to be more moderate to build rapport with other shareholders, rather than excessively voicing demands.[5]

The codetermination model is typically promoted in European countries, especially Germany. The publicly listed companies in Germany have supervisory boards overseeing their executive boards. These supervisory boards must have workforce representatives composing one-third or half of the seats if the companies have more than 500 employees according to Article 4(1) of the German Law on One-Third Participation and German Co-Determination Act of 1976. Article 96(2) of the German Stock Corporation Act also mandates companies with more than 2,000 employees to assign at least 30 percent of board seats to directors of each gender. The worker-elected directors are either employees working at the firms for at least one year, trade union members in the companies, or managerial staff. On top of the supervisory board, workers participation is represented in works councils. Works councils function similarly to trade unions, but their members are not necessarily trade union representatives. The number of work council members is proportionate to the number of employees in the companies, with the exclusion of senior managers (represented by other bodies), the distinguishment of manual and nonmanual employees, and gender equality. Compared to workers representation in the board, workers participation through company shares is less popular as German regulations discourage employee equity-based incentives with tax exemption threshold of €360 (which is significantly lower than the threshold of other countries in Europe, ranging between €2,065 and €6,000. At the "Ownership Day" conferences in 2015 and 2017, companies and experts signed an appeal to increase tax exemption threshold to €3,000, remove dividends and interests taxes, and simplify regulations. According to the appeal, only 14 percent of Germans are shareholders and only half of DAX 30 corporations provide their employees with equity-base incentive plans.[6]

Unlike in most European countries, the shareholder primacy is more popular in the United States. As shareholders' benefits are maximized, no workers are involved in the corporate decision-making process and riskier investment is usually made. Even with the help of labor unions, worker bargaining power is still low if the issues are beyond the terms and conditions of the National Labor Relations Act (NLRA). Amendments to labor laws should be made on both state and federal levels to enable employees' participation, engagement, and impacts on the nomination, and election of corporate board of directors. Recently, there have been proposals from the Reward Work Act and the Accountable Capitalism Act to mandate one-third to 40 percent board seats to be assigned to employees. These proposals encourage the stakeholder theory to replace the shareholder primacy model even though the implementation of codetermination policy can be challenging in the United States.[7]

Environmental Capital

The environmental capital is relevant to environmental impacts of the operation either through the use of natural resources and the nonrenewable, as inputs to the supply chain production or through harmful releases into the environment that could affect bottom-line financial earnings. The environmental capital is crucial to the long-term sustainability of business organizations and their growth and innovation as well as the economic prosperity worldwide in leaving a better environment for next generations. Environmental capital is the natural resources employed and are available to an organization consisting of both renewable resources such as plants and clean air, and nonrenewable assets such as oil and gas. Environmental capital reflects the impact of an organization's operation on the environment including negative values such as contamination, pollution, and desertification. Natural capital is part of the environment including fertile soils, geology, air quality, clean water, and all living organisms, which affect the triple bottom line of people, profit, and the planet. Organizations should preserve the environment and leave a better environment for next generations.

Social Capital

The social capital is relevant to the company's management of relationships with key outside stakeholders including suppliers, customers, local communities, the public, and the government. Social capital is relevant to human rights, responsible business practices, local economic development, customer privacy, and other social matters. The perceived social injustice and unrest in recent years have made social capital more relevant and important to business organizations. Social capital involves the effective functioning of social groups through interpersonal relationships, a shared sense of identity, a shared understanding, shared norms, shared values, trust, cooperation, and reciprocity. Social capital is a measure of the value of resources, both tangible (e.g., public spaces, and private property) and intangible (e.g., actors, HC, and people), and the impact that these relationships have on the resources involved in each relationship, and on larger groups. It is generally seen as a form of capital that produces public goods for a common purpose. Social capital is defined by the OECD as "networks together with shared norms, values and understandings that facilitate co-operation within or among groups."[8] In this definition, the networks are broadly considered as real-world links between groups or individuals including friends, family, colleagues, and local, national, and international communities. The shared values reflect respect for people's safety and security as well as safety, health, and well-being of others.

Social capital has been used to explain the improved performance of diverse groups, the growth of entrepreneurial firms, superior managerial performance, enhanced supply chain relations, the value derived from strategic alliances, and the evolution of communities including positive impacts of human interaction. The positive impacts of social capital are tangible or intangible factors such as useful information, future opportunities, and innovative ideas that can be generated from personal relationships and networks within and outside an organization that enable productive work environment that adds to the bottom-line earnings. Social capital is a set of shared values that enables individuals to work together in a group to effectively achieve a common purpose and goal that help them all. Social capital can be attributed to the factors and characteristics that describe how people are able to band together in society to live harmoniously. In business, social capital can contribute to a company's success and sustainable performance by promoting a sense of shared values, mutual respect, and common goals.

Manufacturing Capital

The manufacturing capital is very broad and consists of issues that pertain to the integration of environmental, human, and social issues into the company's value-creation and value-protection processes. These issues are resource recovery, product innovation, use phase and disposal of products, and efficiency and responsibility in the design. Enhancing accountability and stewardship for the broad base of capitals (financial, manufactured, intellectual, human, social and relationship, and natural) and emphasizing their interdependencies. Manufacturing capital is often used interchangeable with operational capital in describing activities and related resources relevant to customer relationships, trademarks and trade names, supplier relationships, franchises, and licenses. The value of the relationships that a business organization establishes with its customers, and employees can contribute to maintaining manufacturing capital that can be used in the production of goods and services and thus contribute to the long-term sustainability of the business.

Reputational/Trust Capital

The evolution of trust in the now stakeholder era of capitalism has grown increasingly difficult to manage. Research examines global governance and the rule of law with the changing face of leadership, ethical technology, and more.[9] Currently, corporations are instructed to make trust and reputational strength difficult to achieve. Business purpose should be molded into an applied enterprise instead of a static set of promises.

Corporations should begin investing in aligned and effective governance within as well as leadership, employee engagement, and ethical sourcing for green investment decisions and responsible tax policies to build up their reputation and trust capital. Good reputation with stakeholders including shareholders, employees, creditors, customers, suppliers, and communities can take many years to build and can be easily and immediately destroyed with unintentional mistakes and irregularities, and/or intentional fraud to deceive stakeholders.

Corporate culture plays a crucial role in the trust capital. Speaking of culture, Wilcox states that: "There are, however, three proverbial certainties that have developed around corporate culture: (1) We know it when we see it, and worse, we know it most clearly when its failure leads to a crisis. (2) It is a responsibility of the board of directors, defined by their 'tone at the top'. (3) It is the foundation for a company's most precious asset, its reputation." To assess culture of a company, several business metrics such as worker retention, customer satisfaction, legal issues, and so on can be used.[10] Regarding the popularity of shareholder primacy in the United States, the management aims at maximizing the benefits of shareholders. This principal–agent model usually leads to the misalignment of interests, which can be detrimental to trust or reputational capital. Therefore, a reduction in the power of shareholders, or in other words, an increase in power of other stakeholders, especially employees, can be the solution to problems related to integrity in corporate cultures.[11] Moreover, stakeholders now require more transparent communication, which challenges the board of directors to maintain a balance among transparency, confidentiality, and independence.[12]

Intellectual Capital

Intellectual capital refers to the intangible assets that contribute to a company's bottom line earnings as well as long-term sustainability performance and business continuity and survival. Intellectual capital presents resources and intangible assets consisting of organizational investments and processes in developing intellectual capital, the expertise of employees, and all the effort of knowledge contained within the organization. Intellectual capital presents structural capital including the nonphysical infrastructure, processes, databases, and information technology platforms of the organization. Intellectual capital enables other capitals including operational, financial, and HC to function effectively. Structural capital consists of policies, processes, patents, and trademarks, as well as the organization's image, information infrastructure, proprietary software and databases, information technology platforms and innovation, and research and developments.

The business recovery and transformation are essential strategic planning for coping with growing challenges caused by the COVID-19 pandemic. Executives and management team of business organizations under the oversight of the board of directors should consider all possibilities and scenarios under which an organization can survive, recover, and continue sustainable performance by utilizing existing information technology. Business risk assessment and supply chain management can play important roles in the recovery process. Many business organizations have made significant modifications and adjustments to business operations and practices by using intellectual capita and information technology in response to challenges brought on by the COVID-19 pandemic. These organizations are also making changes to their communication, reporting, and control systems using their intellectual capital and information technology and virtual platforms. The finance function is in a better position to evaluate the available instinctual capital and virtual platforms and make suggestion for their adoptions.

Conclusion

Management has traditionally provided stewardship of an organization's resources and its capitals in making strategic decisions that protect interests of all stakeholders. Management as the steward of all business capitals should focus on the long-term interests and well-being of multi-stakeholders is relevant and applicable to corporate governance in the post-COVID-19 era as business organizations are more concerned about safety, health, and well-being of their employees, customers, suppliers, and other stakeholders. Management, as the steward of business resources and related capital discussed in this chapter, has the primary role for improving sustainability performance and managing related risks, maximizing utilization of all capitals from strategic to financial, reputational, manufactured, human, social, and environmental in order to create shared value for all stakeholders. Stakeholder interests in a firm are equity capital, HC, social capital, and compliance capital. Thus, management acts as the steward of strategic capital, financial capital, HC, social capital, and environmental capital and acts as the active and long-term-oriented steward of all stakeholders including shareholders.

Chapter Takeaways

- Employ the stewardship theory with a keen focus on all capitals from strategic to financial, reputational, manufactured, social, environmental, and human in creating accountability and stewardship for all capitals and stakeholders.

- Management, as the steward of business resources, has the primary role for improving sustainability performance and managing related risks, maximizing utilization of all capitals from strategic to financial, reputational, manufactured, human, social, and environmental in order to create shared value for all stakeholders.

- Any environmental initiatives pertaining to reducing pollution levels or saving energy costs may require huge upfront capital expenditures but in the long run will also reduce contingent and actual environmental liabilities.

CHAPTER 3

Shareholder Primacy and Capitalism Model

Executive Summary

The classic profit-maximizing model of publicly traded companies has shaped the role and responsibilities of business organizations in creating value for shareholders. According to this model, a public firm's shareholders elect the board of directors and the board then appoints managers to maximize the firm's profits, and thus maximize the firm's value and shareholders' wealth. The trends emerging in the past few decades, including the focus on protecting the interests of all stakeholders, have raised questions about whether the classic model is still applicable and relevant. According to the shareholder primacy and capitalism model, the primary function of business entities is to maximize shareholder wealth through continuous sustainable economic performance. This chapter addresses the shareholder primacy and capitalism model of business organizations.

Introduction

The goal of companies has evolved from profit maximization, to shareholder wealth enhancement, to creation of shared value for all stakeholders. Traditionally, public companies in the United States have operated under the corporate model known as "shareholder primacy and shareholder capitalism model." This corporate governance model posits that the primary purpose of a corporation is to generate returns for shareholders, and thus managerial decisions and actions should be focused on creating shareholder value. This shareholder primacy model has served investors well in maximizing wealth for them but is being criticized for focusing on generating short-term profits at the expense of long-term sustainability performance innovation, growth, and the social and environmental impacts of corporations. The focus on shareholder wealth creation may not benefit other stakeholders, such as employees, customers, creditors, suppliers, government, society, and the environment. Companies are given rights to operate and generate profits for their shareholders, but with these rights come public interests and societal responsibilities. This chapter presents the shareholder capitalism primacy model and its corporate governance mechanisms and measures.

Shareholder Primacy and Shareholder Capitalism

Corporations as legal entities are incorporated under state law with many privileges, enabling them to raise public capital and create wealth for their owners. Prioritization of shareholder wealth maximization has contributed to wealth inequity and populism in the nation to the extent that the nature, extent, and value of capitalism are being questioned. Policy makers and regulators worldwide also promote the move toward a more balanced-purpose model for public companies. As mentioned previously, Senator Elizabeth Warren introduced the Accountable Capitalism Act in 2018, which if enacted would require public companies in the United States with more than $1 billion in revenues to obtain a federal charter stating the company's "purpose of creating a general public benefit," defined as "a material positive impact on society resulting from the business and operations" of the company.[1] Among the requirements is the mandate that at least 40 percent of the directors of public companies in the United States be elected by employees, and that directors consider the interests of all corporate stakeholders, including customers, suppliers, employees, investors, and the communities in which the corporation operates. Some Democratic congresspersons elected in 2019 advocate social responsibility for corporations. These initiatives by policy makers reflect the larger debate regarding the role of corporations in society that calls into question the fiduciary model of shareholder primacy and advocates move toward stakeholder primacy.

There is less doubt that the capitalism system in the United States has contributed to the economic growth and prosperity for the nation.

However, like any other system, it has its own challenges as many may believe that the capitalism system has not benefited the entire society. Recent focus on environmental and social issues worldwide, many business organizations and their board of directors are paying attention to the growing interest and demand by socially responsible investors, regulators to focus on sustainability factors of performance, risk, and disclosure, and take them into consideration in their pressure to factor into their business and strategic decision making. Profit-oriented business organizations and their board of directors address these sustainability factors in many of their corporate decisions including financial economic sustainability performance and nonfinancial environmental, ethical, social, and governance sustainability performance, their relationships with current or potential employees, customers, and suppliers, their ability to attract capital and investor interests, and to recruit, develop, and retain a talented and motivated workforce. Business organizations should prepare for new sustainability strategic planning to effectively respond to the request from stakeholders for improvement in nonfinancial environmental, social, and governance (ESG) activities and performance as well as the demand by shareholders for improving financial economic sustainability performance in terms of total shareholder return (TSR).

Shareholder Governance

The shareholder aspect of corporate governance is based on the premise that shareholders provide capital to the corporation, which exists for their benefit. It supports the agency theory that the fiduciary duties of corporate directors and executives are to shareholders who have a residual claim on the company's residual assets and cash flows. Shareholders (principals) provide capital to the company, which is run by management (agents). The principal–agent problem exists because corporations are separate entities from their owners—management needs physical capital (investment funds) and investors need skilled human capital (management) to run the company. According to the principal–agent theory, also called the shareholder model of corporate governance, the primary objective of the company is to maximize shareholder wealth and, thus, the role of corporate governance is to ensure the enhancement of shareholder wealth and to align the interests of management with those of the shareholders. The principal–agent problem arises from two factors: the separation of ownership and control, and, most importantly, incomplete contracts or costly enforceable contracts between the agents and principals, known as agency costs. A growing debate in corporate governance is whether corporate gatekeepers including directors and top management team should consider only the interests and wealth of shareholders or should also consider the interests and welfare of all stakeholders such as employees, customers, suppliers, the environment, and local communities when making business decisions. While the corporate governance and agency theory suggest the primary fiduciary duty of corporate gatekeepers is to shareholders, stakeholder governance and stake holder theory advocate corporate gatekeepers' responsibility is to all stakeholders in creating shared value for them. Stakeholder governance has made significant progress in recent years as an alternative to shareholder governance to place more emphasis on impact investing of achieving a desirable rate of returns on investment for shareholders, while generating social and environmental impacts.

The New Paradigm is a roadmap, which is a guide for implicit corporate governance and stewardship partnership between corporations and investors and asset managers to achieve sustainable long-term investment and growth. The premise is based on a defense to attacks from short-term financial activists that impedes long-term financial and economic growth. It is composed of three factors: governance, engagement, and stewardship. Governance relates to the company and its shareholders, and the relationship between them. It also deals with the company's management and board of directors, and the principles in place to create genuine relationships with their shareholders. This can be seen through the company's commitment to long-term business goals as well as effective board oversight. The second factor, engagement, deals with the effective communication and exchange of information between a company and its shareholders. Companies show that they are responsive to shareholder concerns and preferences in an effort to develop the long-term relationship. Finally, stewardship is the accountability of the shareholders, also referred to as the investors and asset managers, to wisely invest the money that supports long-term wealth creation, rather than just meeting short-term goals. These three factors will help management focus on the company, rather than just meeting earnings marks and will benefit the long-term sustainability of a company.

The corporate governance structure should consist of mechanisms (internal and external) designed to effectively align the behavior of management (agents) and its interests with the desires of the principals (shareholders). The agency problem exists when the interests of management and shareholders are not in accord and when there are difficulties in verifying management activities. Agency costs also arise where there is an "information asymmetry" between management and shareholders as well as when the company's board of directors fails to fulfill its fiduciary duties of effectively carrying out its assigned oversight role.

In the real world, the agency problem can never be perfectly solved, and agency costs cannot be eliminated. If complete contracts were feasible and efficiently enforceable, there would be no agency costs, in the sense that investors would have known exactly what management was doing with their funds, and management would know investors' expectations. However, complete contracts are neither feasible nor enforceable, which results in the occurrence of "residual contract rights" of making decisions based on the rights not specified in the contract or based on unforeseen circumstances. The residual contract rights may cause asymmetric information problems as management possesses information that is not disclosed or available to investors, which may result in management entrenchment. Under the shareholder aspect, corporate governance is designed to reduce the agency costs and align the interests of management with those of investors through: (1) providing incentives and opportunities for management to carry out its function effectively, and to maximize shareholder wealth by providing executive compensation plans, ownerships, or stock options; (2) strengthening shareholder rights to monitor, control, and discipline management through enforceable contracts or legal protection; (3) promoting shareholder democracy; (4) improving the vigilance of the board's oversight function; (5) holding directors accountable and liable for the fulfillment of their fiduciary duties; and (6) improving the effectiveness of both internal corporate governance mechanisms (board of directors and internal controls) and external corporate governance mechanisms (external audit, monitoring, and regulatory functions).

Shareholders as owners of public companies should be attentive and protect their investment by attending shareholders annual meetings (in person and/or virtual) to vote on corporate governance issues as reflected in management and shareholders resolutions. The 2019 proxy paper issued by the advisory firm Glass Lewis identifies many shareholder corporate governance initiatives that are addressed in all chapters in this module.[2] Shareholders play a crucial role in corporate governance through their voting right and engagements in meetings and discussions with the board of directors and management. These engagements enable shareholders to submit their governance proposals at the annual meetings. In the United States, shareholders need to own at least 1 percent or $2,000 of a company's share to submit a proposal for inclusion in proxy statements.[3]

The shareholder-driven aspect of corporate governance is based on agency theory and the shareholder primacy model. Under this aspect of corporate governance, the main focus is on maximizing shareholder wealth and as such all corporate governance measures and reforms are aimed at protecting interests of investors regardless of the impacts of business operations on the well-being of other stakeholders, such as employees, customers, creditors, suppliers, government, society, and the environment. Shareholder-driven corporate governance will draw the attention of directors and management to maximizing profit and creating value for shareholders but may not serve the purpose of creating shared value for all stakeholders. Corporations and their directors and officers typically focus primarily on maximizing shareholder wealth in the short term by engaging in earnings management in beating analysts' forecast expectations at the expense of long-term sustainable performance and protecting interests of employees, suppliers, customers, society, and the environment.

Shareholder primacy is an owner-centric form of corporate governance that focuses on maximization of shareholder wealth before considering the interests of other stakeholders, such as employees, customers, society, community, consumers, and the environment. The debate between a shareholder primacy and a stakeholder primacy has been extensive, long-lasting, and inconclusive. Proponents of shareholder primacy suggest that *corporations* should focus on shareholder wealth maximization, while advocates of stakeholder primacy indicate the importance of corporations in generating shared value for all stakeholders. Some of the shortcomings of shareholder primacy are given as follows:

The tendency to focus on short-term performance to achieve the short-term targets of maximizing shareholder wealth.
Unwillingness to take on risks and invest in new technologies research and development.

The shareholder model of corporate governance is considered to be an impediment to corporate social responsibility (CSR) and sustainability. Under the shareholder model, management is commonly constrained from taking CSR initiatives and expenditures that may be viewed as inconsistent with the economic interests of shareholders. Shareholder-driven corporate governance suggests that shareholders are attentive in looking after their investments by governing the corporation that they own and by protecting their interests while also involving in the governance of the company. Shareholder-driven governance captures both actual and potential governance strategies to: (1) minimize the concerns relating to management and board entrenchment; and (2) respond to the shift in the balance of power within public corporations between the board of directors, management, and investors, particularly investor activism. The Dodd Frank "say-on-pay" reforms of 2010 are a prime example of an increased move toward shareholder-driven governance in influencing executive compensation and in separating the roles of board chair and chief executive officer (CEO). However, the extent of shareholder-driven governance depends on the sizes and types of shareholders. It is expected that institutional investors (pension funds, mutual funds, and hedge funds) engage more in corporate governance than individual retail investors because of the level of their sophistication and resources.

Shareholders play an important role in corporate governance by electing directors who appoint management to make day-to-day business decisions for public companies. In addition, shareholders vote on many important issues that can create value for them. Generally, at annual shareholder meetings, shareholders vote for or against candidates for director positions, obtain detail information regarding executive compensation plans, put forth proposals for consideration by other shareholders, and attend special shareholder meetings to vote on important corporate structure matters (mergers and acquisitions). Shareholders have options of casting their votes at the meetings in person or "by proxy" including online, by mail, or by phone. Shareholders play an important role in corporate governance by exercising their voting rights and engaging in meetings and discussions with the board and management. This engagement has become increasingly crucial when shareholders submit their own proposals at the companies' annual meetings. Proactive participation and monitoring by shareholders in the company they own is an important component of effective corporate governance. The shareholder theory of corporate governance is derived from the agency aspect of corporations and is based on the concept that the primary objective of corporations is to create shareholder value, and thus the purpose of corporate governance is to align management interests with those of shareholders. According to the agency theory, shareholders (principals) hire management (agent) to manage the corporation for the benefit of owners. There may be conflicts of interest between management and shareholders. Thus, the corporate governance structure and measures are designed to focus on the process of directing and managing the business and affairs of the corporation to achieve its objective of creating shareholder value. The shareholder theory of corporate governance concentrates on role of the board of directors and management to manage corporate activities in achieving financial performance that maximize shareholder wealth.

Agency/shareholder theory focuses on risk sharing and agency problems between shareholders and management by suggesting that the interests of principals (owners) and their agents (executives) are often not aligned. Thus, in the context of agency theory, the role of corporate governance is to align interests of management with those of shareholders. Moral hazards can occur in the presence of information asymmetry where the agent (management) acting on behalf of the principal (shareholders) knows more about its actions and/or intentions than the principal does due to a lack of effective corporate governance in properly monitoring management. The implications of agency/shareholder theory for corporate governance are that management incentives and activities often focus on short-term earnings targets and self-serving of maximizing executive compensation rather than improving long-term performance in creating shareholder value. Thus, corporate governance measures should be in place to ensure management focus on creating shareholder value.

Director Fiduciary Duties

Directors have fiduciary duties of care and loyalty that they must uphold. These duties require the directors to use informed, deliberate decision-making and to act on a disinterested and independent basis when making decisions. They are required to use good faith and judgement to act in the best interest of the company and the stockholders they represent. A "Roadmap" to satisfying fiduciary duties should be followed. With it, directors should be well-advised and properly informed, using all material information available to them. They must be comfortable with all processes, keep confidential information confidential, be able to weigh out risks and rewards and compare them to alternatives, and be able to respond appropriately to all issues. Finally, they must ultimately act in good faith and make decisions on what they believe is in the best interest for the company.

A big responsibility that directors must deal with is effective oversight over the company and its risk management. Protocols to monitor and avoid risk, as well as comply with laws and regulations must be put in place to avoid a breach in fiduciary duties. To do this, a good board process must be established. Having a good board process in place creates an appropriate framework for any situation, while also recording how situations were handled and serving as evidence for the director's completion of the fiduciary duties. This is all very important because if director is sent to court, the burden is now on the plaintiff to provide evidence of gross negligence regarding a director's fiduciary duties, due to the business judgment rule. This rule, along with reliance with company records, indemnification and expense advancement, exculpation of certain personal liabilities, and directors and officers (D&O) liability insurance are provisions that help directors satisfy their fiduciary duties and protect that from possible accusations of breach.

The World Economic Forum recommends business organizations to move from the traditional model of corporate governance and shareholder capitalism to the model of stakeholder governance and stakeholder capitalism.[4] Under the stakeholder governance model, the fiduciary duty of the board of directors is extended to all stakeholders including shareholders, employees, customers, suppliers, communities, society, and the environment. The stakeholder governance will be examined in the next chapter.

Conclusion

The shareholder aspect of corporate governance implies that shareholders, by virtue of their ownership investment in the company, are entitled to direct and monitor the company's business and affairs. Shareholders influence corporate governance by exercising their right to elect directors, who then appoint management to run the company. Directors and officers, as agents of the company, act as trustees on behalf of shareholders, and their primary responsibilities and fiduciary duties are to shareholders. While directors' and officers' legal fiduciary duties are only extended to shareholders who invested in the company, they may have many nonfiduciary duties to other stakeholders, who may have various interests and claims to the company's welfare. Shareholders' rights, including the right to elect, the right to put propositions before the annual shareholder meetings, and the right to reliable and accurate financial information, are legally enforceable, and offending directors and officers can be brought to justice through the courts. Corporate purpose is now changing as there are more support for stakeholder governance and stakeholder theory in creating shared value for all stakeholders and in maximizing stakeholder welfare than just creating shareholder value and in maximizing shareholder wealth.

Chapter Takeaways

- Shareholder primacy focuses on creating value for shareholders.
- Shareholder capitalism has served U.S. companies well.
- Shareholder capitalism needs to be modified and broadened.
- Under shareholder primacy, the only fiduciary responsibility of the board of directors is to shareholders in protecting their interests.

- Stakeholder governance and stakeholder theory suggest business organizations should create shared value for all stakeholders.
- Corporate purpose should be focused on maximizing welfare value for all stakeholders than just maximizing shareholder wealth.

CHAPTER 4

Stakeholder Primacy and Capitalism Model

Executive Summary

The emerging concept of profit-with-purpose corporations suggests that public companies should have the dual mission of profit-making function of creating shareholder value, while protecting interests of other stakeholders through their social benefit function. It appears there is a move away from pure shareholder primacy to stakeholder primacy of profit-with-purpose corporations. It appears that European and Asian companies are moving closer to the concept of stakeholder primacy than their counterparts in North America. This chapter presents the stakeholder capitalism primacy model with the main objective function of creating shared value for all stakeholders.

Introduction

In the past several decades, there has been a movement worldwide toward the stakeholder primacy model of corporations and related corporate governance measures intended to fundamentally rebalance power among stakeholders. The stakeholder primacy model holds that public companies should focus on corporate purposes beyond shareholder value, and thus maintains that corporate governance measures and corporate decision-making should also consider every stakeholder who provides capital (including financial, operational, human, societal, and environmental) and contributes to corporate success. The Board's Role Under Stakeholder Primacy/Capitalism as Opposed to Shareholder Primacy/Capitalism is to oversee managerial function of focusing on the long-term sustainability performance, effectively communicating sustainability performance information to all stakeholders. The board should be informed and understand the stakeholder objectives, rationales for focusing on sustainability factors of performance, risk and disclosure, and managerial strategic planning, sustainable operational performance, and executive compensation in promoting long-term corporate value. This chapter presents the stakeholder capitalism primacy model and its governance mechanisms and measures with the main objective function of creating shared value for all stakeholders.

Stakeholder Capitalism Primacy

The goal of companies has evolved from profit maximization, to shareholder wealth enhancement, to creation of shared value for all stakeholders. The magnitude of ESG (environmental, social, and governance) sustainability-focused investment is now more than $20 trillion. ESG funds require that corporations define their purpose of generating financial returns and achieving social and environmental impacts. For many years, the focus on profit maximization for shareholders worked in U.S. financial markets. Globalization, technological advances, and often disruption have forced corporations to focus on the short-termism of meeting or beating analysts' forecast expectations. However, corporations are now facing pressures from social activists and stakeholders to pay attention to the interests of customers, suppliers, employees, society, and the environment, among others, to create shared value for all stakeholders. In August 2019, the Business Roundtable issued a statement, signed by the CEOs of 187 major public companies, in which they committed to "lead their companies to the benefit of all stakeholders," and to "deliver value" not just to shareholders but also to employees, customers, suppliers, and communities.[1] The World Economic Forum (WEF) highly recommends companies to move from the traditional model of "shareholder capitalism" to the model of "stakeholder capitalism."[2] The WEF supports the concept of stakeholder governance in the context of stakeholder capitalism and has developed the stakeholder governance principles to protect interests of shareholders, employees, customers, suppliers, governments, and society as part of its COVID Action Platform.[3]

The Rise of Stakeholders/in Action/Compensation

At these times, there is a rise in stakeholder action, which grows with the increasing pressure for companies to respect all stakeholders versus the shareholder. The digital age has created a new way of work, shifting the service economy to become more automated, which results in the need for more skilled, talented, and experienced workers. Employees, customers, suppliers, and even the local and global communities are now viewed as major stakeholders, as well as central to the long-term success and sustainability of a company. Even during trying times such as the COVID-19 pandemic and other short-term pressures on companies, the key to success will remain with the support of all major stakeholders and the integrated ecosystem the firm is involved in.[4]

Stakeholders are individuals or groups who affect the company's strategic decisions, operations, and performance, and are also affected by its decisions or activities. Traditionally, shareholders have been the primary users of the company's financial reports, which reflect the company's financial condition and the results of operations. While shareholders are still the primary recipient of the company's reports on economic performance, stakeholders are now becoming more engaged and interested in the company's multiple bottom lines (MBL) performance on a variety of economic, governance, ethical, social, and environmental issues. Shareholders' initiatives, proposals, and resolutions on environmental and social issues are being considered by the board of directors and incorporated into the corporate governance structure.

Stakeholder theory of corporate governance is gaining support in the aftermath of the 2007–2009 global financial crisis and the move toward business sustainability. Stakeholder theory requires the following: (1) identification of all stakeholders who affect and are affected by the organization's business and affairs including investors, creditors, customers, employees, suppliers, society, and the environment; (2) determination of rights, authorities, responsibilities, and accountability of each stakeholder; (3) development of a systematic process to ensure proper accountability for the stewardship of the organization's resources and capitals; and (4) establishment of a fair system of rewards based on the risk taken by stakeholders. Under the stakeholder theory of corporate governance, the corporate primary objective is to achieve sustainable financial and non-financial performance in creating shared value for all stakeholders.

Several initiatives have been undertaken in moving away from shareholder primacy and toward stakeholder primacy under this new corporate governance model, including the following:[5]

1. The board's fiduciary duty should be extended to all stakeholders, and the board of directors should be accountable to all stakeholders, not just share owners.

2. Corporate purpose statements should specifically state that corporations positively benefit society in the context of creating shared value for all stakeholders.

3. Multiple stakeholders, including employees, should be represented on corporate boards.

4. Large corporations should be required to be organized under federal charters, to facilitate governance reform accountability that requires responsibility to all stakeholders.

5. Legislative acts and regulatory mandates.

The future of the corporation has been the subject of the extensive debate in the business and academic community. Colin Mayer's *Prosperity: Better Business Makes the Greater Good* challenges the fundamentals of business thinking and purpose, and criticizes many businesses for causing inequality, poor innovation, environmental degradation, and low growth.[6] The book also suggests that the corporation of the future can make capitalism sustainable by establishing and implementing corporate governance measures and reforms that promote an alignment of corporate conduct with social purpose, ensuring that companies' strategic plans and their governance, measurement, and incentive systems as related to the environment, culture ownership, and other social issues, are appropriate for these purposes.[7] The future of the corporation will focus on aligning corporate goals with social interests, an approach promoted by the British Academy, the UK's national body for the social sciences and the humanities.[8] In moving toward the implementation of this concept of the future of the corporation, business organizations should (1) define their purpose with the goal of aligning the maximizing of shareholder value with social purpose, (2) specify their commitments to all stake-holders, (3) design mechanisms to uphold their commitments, and (4) disclose their accountability with respect to ownership, governance, and performance measurements in achieving their stated purposes.[9] This view of the corporation, based on stakeholder primacy rather than shareholder primacy, promotes the main goal of creating shared value for all stake-holders rather than that of merely maximizing shareholder wealth.

Stakeholder Governance

Corporate governance effectiveness has been the main focus of business organizations and their stakeholders including shareholders, employees, suppliers, customers, and communities. The stakeholder governance recognizes the importance of business survival and continuity in the short term as well as sustainable value creation for all shareholders in the long term as corporate strategy. The stakeholder model of corporate governance focuses on the broader view of the company with purpose and profit as the nexus of contracts among all corporate governance partici-pants with the common goal of creating shared value for all stakeholders. The stakeholder model concentrates on maximization of wealth for all stakeholders, including the following: (1) contractual participants such as shareholders, creditors, suppliers, customers, and employees; and (2) social constituents including the local community; society and global partners; local, state, and federal governments; and environmental matters. Under this view, public companies must be socially responsible—good citizens granted the use of the nation's physical and human capital, managed in the public interest and leave a better environment for the next genera-tions. Thus, the performance of public companies is measured in terms of key financial indicators (earnings, market share, and stock price), social indicators (employment, customer satisfaction, and fair trading with sup-pliers), ethical indicators (proper business culture and business code of conduct), and environmental indicators (antipollution and preservation of natural resources). Public companies' performance is measured based on financial impacts as well as social and environmental impacts.

Stakeholders have a reciprocal relationship and interaction with a firm in the sense that they contribute to the firm's value creation, and the firm's performance affects their well-being. Stakeholder theory applies to all managerial processes in the sense that the synergy and integration among all elements of the business model and its processes are essential in achieving overall sustainable performance objectives. From the stakeholder's perspective, an organization is viewed as part of a network consisting of groups that work together to achieve the network/system goals. However, management may take actions to improve sustainability performance that benefit stakeholders (shareholders) who have the power to influence its compensation. The application of stakeholder theory to corporate governance, and thus management processes suggests that a company should be viewed as a nexus of all stakeholders. Corporate stakeholders are shareholders, creditors, customers, suppliers, employees, government, competitors, the environment, and society. Under stakeholder theory, management's role is to improve sustainable performance in creating shared value for all stakeholders. The stakeholder governance paradigm requires a new set of guiding principles driven by shared value concept, new governance functions redefining the fiduciary duties of directors and executives to all stakeholders, and a new set of corporate governance measures to ensure its effectiveness.

The board should also provide oversight, insight, and foresight function on the achievement of both financial economic sustainability performance (ESP) and nonfinancial environmental, ethical, social, and governance (EESG) sustainability performance driven from financial, human, social, manufacturing capitals as well as innovation, culture, corporate governance, and ESG initiatives.[10] The Board's Role Under Stakeholder Primacy/Capitalism as Opposed to Shareholder Primacy/Capitalism is to oversee managerial function of focusing on the long-term sustainability performance, effectively communicating sustainability performance information to all stakeholders. The board should be informed and understand the stakeholder objectives, rationales for focusing on sustainability factors of performance, risk and disclosure, and managerial strategic planning, sustainable operational performance, and executive compensation in promoting long-term corporate value. The board should also provide oversight, insight, and foresight function on the achievement of both financial ESP and nonfinancial EESG performance driven from financial, human, social, manufacturing capitals, as well as innovation, culture, corporate governance, and ESG initiatives.[11] The financial and nonfinancial key performance indicators (KPIs) should be identified, measured, and disclosed through metrics that reflect corporate value, long-term investment, and innovation on EESG initiatives. In general, the five sustainability oversight functions of the board of directors are given as follows:[12]

1. Refocusing on the long term: Companies and their investors, board of directors, and executives should focus on long-term sustainable goals and achievements than short-term gains as the short-term focus may discourage them to invest in research, technology, innovation, and ESG initiatives.
2. Identifying, measuring, and disclosing key drivers of long-term value: The four major drivers of long-term value are:
   • Talent—Employees can significantly influence a company's ability to generate long-term value by implementing its strategy, improving operational effectiveness, and developing new ideas for success and growth. The three areas that the talent can result in sustainability achievement of long-term performance and related metrics and disclosures are human capital development, management, engagement, and turnover; organizational culture and related employee views and data; employee health programs, participation, and impact on productivity.
   • Innovation and consumer trends—Companies should ensure that their innovation is meeting evolving demands by customers and other stakeholders and continuously interact with them to assess their innovation and develop related metrics to measure and disclose their success in addressing overall innovation strategy performance and metrics, consumer trust scores, and consumer health impacts.
   • Society and the environment—The concept of impact investing of focusing on both financial returns and social and environmental impacts of business organization is gaining momentum with investors. Companies should identify and measure their impacts on society and the environment by linking their strategic goals to the United Nations' Sustainability Development Goals (SDGs).

- Corporate governance—There has been much progress on corporate governance and its measures in the past two decades. However, corporate governance is a process (journey) that needs continuous improvements. Areas of improvements in corporate governance are given as follows: robust and continuous evaluation of the board effectiveness, its composition, diversity, and dynamics; board oversight function in creating value and protecting value; and corporate governance reporting in properly disclosing its success and long-term performance.

3. Developing company-specific sustainability metrics: Sustainability metrics on both financial ESP and nonfinancial EESG should be tailored to the companies' mission, purpose, culture, strategy, objectives, and operating activities.

4. Identifying sustainability issues that drive value: The Sustainability Accounting Standards Board (SASB) released its new standards in November 2018, which are intended to enable business organizations in different industries to identify, measure, report, and manage their sustainability factors of performance, risk, and disclosure. These standards can be tailored to a particular company in a specific industry culture and operations that can have long-term material financial impacts. The SASB identifies 28 sustainability factors and issues broadly organized into the following five groups: the environment, social capita, human capital, business model and innovation, and leadership and governance.[13]

The stakeholder governance concept with the focus on stakeholders has recently been debated among policy makers, regulators, investors, business community, and the accounting profession with both discussion of positive impacts of benefiting all stakeholders and imposing additional costs on shareholders and society.[14] However, the WEF advocates the stakeholder governance concept and has established the stakeholder governance principles to protect interests of all stakeholders including shareholders, employees, customers, suppliers, governments, and society.[15] the International Business Council (IBC) of the WEF, in collaboration with the big 4 accounting firms, has released its final recommendations for a set of globally accepted, standardized, and industry-oriented ESG sustainability performance metrics and disclosures.[16] These recommendations are intended to provide guiding principles for focusing on the ESG sustainability factors of performance, risk, and disclosures on governance, people, planet, and prosperity.

The IBC/WEF framework defines a set of "Stakeholder Capitalism Metrics" for business organization worldwide to use and publicly report their ESG sustainability factors of performance, risk, and disclosure on a more standardized, comparable, and consistent metrics. These metrics can also be used to examine a company's compliance and contributions toward achieving the SDGs. These suggested guiding principles, recommendations, and related metrics reflect the insight from, and views of many constituencies including IBC members and nonmembers, workshops, and meetings with investors and across industry sectors, as well as conversations with and inputs from regulators, stock exchanges, and standard-setters. The recommendations encourage companies to report on their core ESG metrics using a "disclose or explain" like corporate governance reporting of "comply or explain non-compliance" approach by focusing on a "materiality test" of reporting ESG information that is material, important, relevant, and/or critical to long-term shared value creation for all stakeholders.

These recommendations emphasize materiality of ESG disclosure that are relevant subject to confidentiality constraints, data availability, legal prohibitions, or other considerations. Companies are encouraged to disclose ESG information where relevant and possible, in their annual reports, proxy statements, or in a separate stand-alone integrated sustainability report. Business organizations that choose to comply with the recommended core metrics would disclose ESG sustainability factors of performance, risk, and related metrics relevant to (1) governance issues including corporate purpose; quality of governing body (e.g., the board of directors and related audit, compensation, and nominating committees); composition, competencies, and diversity of board committees; stakeholder engagement; oversight and disclosure of material risks and opportunities, pertaining to economic, environmental, social, and governance issues; and ethical behavior and practices (anticorruption; fraud prevention's internal and external mechanisms for ethics advice and reporting); (2) people including dignity and equality (diversity, inclusion,

and fair compensation); health, safety, and well-being; skills for the future
(training hours and expenses); (3) planet including climate change and
climate-related financial disclosures, nature loss, and freshwater availability; and (4) prosperity including employment and wealth generation,
innovation and growth through offering the best products and services,
(R&D expenses), and community and social vitality. Exhibit 4.1 presents
the IBC/WEF's recommended ESG factors of governance, planet, people,
and prosperity, and their related metrics.

*Exhibit 4.1 Recommendations of IBC/WEF for ESG sustainability
factors and four pillars under stakeholder governance*

Governance	People	Planet	Prosperity
• Principles of governance • Governing purpose (setting purpose). • Quality of governing body (board directors, related committees, and committee composition, competencies and diversity). • Stakeholder engagement (material issues/ topics/ factors impacting stakeholders). • Ethical behavior (anticorruption; fraud prevention; internal and external mechanisms for ethics advice and reporting). • Risk and opportunity oversight (integrating risk and opportunities into corporate culture, business environment, and processes).	• Dignity, inclusion, and equality (fair compensation pay gap disclosures; discrimination and harassment and collective bargaining coverage of workforce and suppliers). • Health, safety, and well-being (workplace safety; access to health care; cost of occupational incidents; workplace fatalities; well-being programs; absentee rate). • Skills for the future (training hours and expenses; unfilled skilled positions; investment and effectiveness of training).	• Climate change (greenhouse gas emissions; The Task Force on Climate-Related Financial Disclosures (TCFD) implementation). • Nature loss (land use and ecological sensitivity). • Freshwater availability (water withdrawal and consumption in water stress areas). • Nature loss (land use for plant, animal or mineral commodities). • Air and water pollution • Solid waste • Resource availability	• Employment and wealth generation (employee turnover; economic contribution and value generation; infrastructure investments and services; indirect economic impacts). • Innovation of better products and services (total R&D expense/cost; social benefits generated; share of revenue from recently launched products). • Community and social vitality (taxes paid; Total Social Investment; additional tax disclosures).

Stakeholder governance principles provide guidelines for corporate gatekeepers and participants from the board of directors to executives, investors, legal counsel, and financial advisors and auditors to effectively discharge their responsibility and fulfill their accountability. Stakeholder governance guiding principles are advancing and intended to provide a basic framework and foundation for an effective governance in protecting interests of all stakeholders and as such they are applicable to all types and sizes of organizations. The primary oversight function of the board of directors under stakeholder governance is to protect interests of multistakeholders by appointing competent, accountable, ethical, and responsible executives to manage the business for the benefit of all stakeholders. Regulators worldwide should promulgate proactive, cost-efficient, effective, and scalable rules and regulation to protect the interests of all stakeholders. Internal and external governance mechanisms should be established to achieve the organizational purposes, mission, vision, values, and goals. Internal mechanisms consist of a vigilant board of directors in overseeing the organization's purpose, mission, objectives, and strategies, executives' commitments to implement proper strategies to minimize the negative impacts and maximize positive impacts of the organization's activities, operations, and performance. External mechanisms established by policy makers, regulators, and standard-setters can play an important role in stakeholder governance in establishing applicable laws, regulations, rules, and standards, which are intended to benefit all stakeholders and protect their interests.

The new stakeholder governance paradigm recognizes the importance of short-term and long-term sustainable value creation for all shareholders by viewing governance as coordination and collaboration among all corporate governance participants from shareholders to boards of directors, executives, and other stakeholders to achieve financial ESP and nonfinancial EESG sustainability performance in creating shared value for all stakeholders. The emerging new stakeholder governance enables global business organizations worldwide to better realize their responsibility for the safety, health, and well-being of shareholders employees, customers, and suppliers, as well as redefine their business purpose of achieving financial ESP and nonfinancial EESG sustainability performance. The new stakeholder governance paradigm requires a new coherent set of guiding principles provided by the WEF driven by shared value concept, new governance functions redefining the fiduciary duties of directors and executives to all stakeholders, and a new set of internal and external governance mechanisms.

Conclusion

There has been a move toward the stakeholder capitalism and primacy model to ensure long-term sustainability of business corporations in generating desired financial returns for their shareholders while protecting interests of all stakeholders. Stakeholders such as employees, creditors, customer, suppliers, social responsibility activists, and communities, who are affected by and can affect the success of the company, do not have the right to direct or monitor the company. Nonetheless, the interests of stakeholders are protected under the contract and tort laws and the stakeholder capitalism and primacy model. Stakeholder capitalism and its stakeholder governance concept are intended to benefit all stakeholders. The stakeholder governance paradigm including guiding principles, functions, and measures should assist governance participants from the board of directors to management, accountants, auditors, legal counsel, stakeholders to address, and take actions in protecting interests of all stakeholders. Stakeholder governance is driven from the stakeholder primacy concept with focus on creating and protecting shared value for all stakeholders. Business organizations worldwide should modify their corporate governance to ensure protecting interests of all stakeholders. Business organizations should understand the move toward the stakeholder governance with focus on sustainability factors of performance, risk and disclosure, and integration of these factors into corporate culture and business environment as well as managerial policies, decisions, and processes to protect interests of their stakeholders.

Chapter Takeaways

- Business organizations should generate shared value for all stakeholders.
- Stakeholders include shareholders, employees, customers, creditors, suppliers, communities, society, and the environment.
- There is a move away from the traditional model of shareholder capitalism and primacy toward the stakeholder capitalism and primacy model.

Notes

Chapter 1

1. Business Roundtable (BRT) (2019).
2. Harvard Law School Forum on Corporate Governance. An Alternative Paradigm to "On the Purpose of the Corporation" (2020).
3. Harvard Law School Forum on Corporate Governance. On the Purpose of the Corporation (2020).
4. Investor Responsibility Research Center Institute (IRRCi) (2018).
5. Global Impact Investing Network (GIIN) (2019).
6. European Union (EU) Directive (2014).
7. BRT (2019).
8. Rezaee and Fogarty (2019).
9. Ibid.
10. Ibid.
11. Harvard Law School Forum on Corporate Governance (2020).
12. Harvard Law School Forum on Corporate Governance (2019).
13. Harvard Law School Forum on Corporate Governance (2019).
14. Harvard Law School Forum on Corporate Governance (2020).
15. Ibid.
16. Harvard Law School Forum on Corporate Governance (2020).
17. KPMG (2020).
18. Fried (November 2019).
19. Bebchuk and Tallarita (March 2020).
20. Mayer (June 2020).

Chapter 2

1. The Committee of Sponsoring Organizations of the Treadway Commission (COSO) and the World Business Council for Sustainable Development (WBCSD) (2018).
2. International Integrated Reporting Committee (IIRC) (2013).

3. IIRC (2013).
4. Organization of Economic Co-Operation and Development (OECD) (2018).
5. MIT Economics (2020).
6. Harvard Law School Forum on Corporate Governance (2020).
7. Harvard Law School Forum on Corporate Governance (2019).
8. OECD (2019).
9. Harvard Law School Forum on Corporate Governance (2020).
10. Harvard Law School Forum on Corporate Governance (2020).
11. Harvard Law School Forum on Corporate Governance (2019).
12. Harvard Law School Forum on Corporate Governance (2020).

Chapter 3

1. Warren (2018).
2. Warren (2018).
3. Ibid.
4. Davos (2020).

Chapter 4

1. Business Roundtable (2019).
2. Davos (2020).
3. The World Economic Forum (WEF) (2020).
4. Harvard Law School Forum on Corporate Governance. Burchman and O'Toole (2020).
5. Palladino and Karlsson (2018).
6. Mayer (2018).
7. Ibid.
8. Mayer (2018).
9. Ibid.
10. Klemash, Smith, and Doyle (2019).
11. Klemash, Smith, and Doyle (2019).
12. Ibid.
13. Sustainability Accounting Standards Board (SASB) (2018).
14. Rezaee and Rezaee (2020).
15. Ibid.
16. World Economic Forum (WEF) (2020).

References

Bebchuk, L., and R. Tallarita. March 2020. "The Illusory Promise of Stakeholder Governance." *Harvard Law School Forum on Corporate Governance.* Available at https://corpgov.law.harvard.edu/2020/03/02/the-illusory-promise-of-stakeholder-governance/

Business Roundtable BRT (2019)."Statement on the Purpose of a Corporation." Available at https://opportunity.businessroundtable.org/wp-content/uploads/2019/09/BRT-Statement-on-the-Purpose-of-a-Corporation-with-Signatures-1.pdf

Business Roundtable (BRT). August 19, 2019. "Statement on the Purpose of a Corporation." Available at https://opportunity.businessroundtable.org/wp-content/uploads/2019/09/BRT-Statement-on-the-Purpose-of-a-Corporation-with-Signatures-1.pdf

Business Roundtable. 2019. "Business Roundtable Redefines the Purpose of a Corporation to Promote An Economy That Serves All Americans." https://businessroundtable.org/business-roundtable-redefines-the-purpose-of-a-corporation-to-promote-an-economy-that-serves-all-americans

Davos, M. 2020. "The Universal Purpose of a Company in the Fourth Industrial Revolution." https://weforum.org/agenda/2019/12/davos-manifesto-2020-the-universal-purpose-of-a-company-in-the-fourth-industrial-revolution/

European Union (EU) Directive. 2014/95/EU. "Directive 2014/95/EU of the European Parliament and of the Council amending Directive 2013/34/EU as Regards Disclosure of Non-Financial and Diversity Information by Certain Large Undertakings And Groups." Available at https://eur-lex.europa.eu/legal-content/EN/TXT/PDF/?uri=CELEX:32014L0095&from=EN

Fried, J.M. November 2019. "The Roundtable's Stakeholderism Rehetoric is Empty, Thankfully." *Harvard Law School Forum on Corporate Governance.* Available at https://corpgov.law.harvard.edu/2019/11/22/the-roundtables-stakeholderism-rhetoric-is-empty-thankfully/

Global Impact Investing Network (GIIN). 2019. "White Paper." Available at https://thegiin.org/research/publication/impinv-survey-2019

Harvard Law School Forum on Corporate Governance. 2019. "A Common-Sense Approach to Corporate Purpose, ESG and Sustainability." Available at https://corpgov.law.harvard.edu/2019/10/26/a-common-sense-approach-to-corporate-purpose-esg-and-sustainability/

Harvard Law School Forum on Corporate Governance. 2019. "The Effects of Shareholder Primacy, Publicness, and "Privateness" on Corporate Cultures." Available at https://corpgov.law.harvard.edu/2019/09/23/the-effects-of-shareholder-primacy-publicness-and-privateness-on-corporate-cultures/

Harvard Law School Forum on Corporate Governance. 2019. "What Does the Growth of Impact Investing Mean?" Available at https://corpgov.law.harvard.edu/2019/11/10/what-does-the-growth-of-impact-investing-mean/

Harvard Law School Forum on Corporate Governance. 2019. "Worker Representation on U.S. Corporate Boards." Available at https://corpgov.law.harvard.edu/2019/12/30/worker-representation-on-u-s-corporate-boards/#:~:text=Thus%2C%20a%20federal%20legislation%20solution, one%2Dthird%20of%20board%20seats

Harvard Law School Forum on Corporate Governance. 2020. "An Alternative Paradigm to On the Purpose of the Corporation." Available at https://corpgov.law.harvard.edu/2020/06/04/an-alternative-paradigm-to-on-the-purpose-of-the-corporation/

Harvard Law School Forum on Corporate Governance. 2020. "Corporate Purpose and Culture." Available at https://corpgov.law.harvard.edu/2020/02/21/corporate-purpose-and-culture/

Harvard Law School Forum on Corporate Governance. 2020. "For Whom Corporate Leaders Bargain." Available at https://corpgov.law.harvard.edu/2020/08/25/for-whom-corporate-leaders-bargain/

Harvard Law School Forum on Corporate Governance. 2020. "On the Purpose of the Corporation." Available at https://corpgov.law.harvard.edu/2020/05/27/on-the-purpose-of-the-corporation/

Harvard Law School Forum on Corporate Governance. 2020. "The Evolution of Trust in the Era of Stakeholder Capitalism." Available at https://corpgov.law.harvard.edu/2020/04/23/the-evolution-of-trust-in-the-era-of-stakeholder-capitalism/

Harvard Law School Forum on Corporate Governance. 2020. "Towards a Common Language for Sustainable Investing." Available at https://corpgov.law.harvard.edu/2020/01/22/towards-a-common-language-for-sustainable-investing/

Harvard Law School Forum on Corporate Governance. 2020. "Why and How Capitalism Needs to Be Reformed." Available at https://corpgov.law.harvard.edu/2020/10/13/why-and-how-capitalism-needs-to-be-reformed/

Harvard Law School Forum on Corporate Governance. 2020. "Worker Participation: Employee Ownership And Representation." Available at https://corpgov.law.harvard.edu/2020/01/23/worker-participation-employee-ownership-and-representation/#:~:text=There%20are%20two%20main%20forms,on%20the%20board%20of%20directors.

Harvard Law School Forum on Corporate Governance. Burchman and O'Toole. 2020. "An Inflection Point for Stakeholder Capitalism." Available at https://corpgov.law.harvard.edu/2020/08/22/an-inflection-point-for-stakeholder-capitalism/

International Integrated Reporting Committee IIRC. 2013."IIRC Consultative Draft." IIRC Consultative Draft Section 3.12; page 19. http://theiirc.org/consultationdraft2013/

Investor Responsibility Research Center Institute (IRRCi). 2018. "Measuring Effectiveness: Roadmap to Assessing System-level and SDG Investing." https://corpgov.law.harvard.edu/2018/04/19/measuring-effectiveness-roadmap-to-assessing-system-level-and-sdg-investing/

Klemash, S., J.C. Smith, and R. Doyle. 2019. "Stakeholder Capitalism for Long-Term Value Creation." *Harvard Law School on Corporate Governance and Financial Regulation.* Available at https://corpgov.law.harvard.edu/2019/06/13/stakeholder-capitalism-for-long-term-value-creation/

KPMG. 2020. "The Time Has Come; the KPMG Survey of Sustainability Reporting 2020." Available at https://home.kpmg/xx/en/home/insights/2020/11/the-time-has-come-survey-of-sustainability-reporting.html

Mayer, C. 2018. "Prosperity: Better Business Makes the Greater Good." https://moralmarkets.org/book/prosperity-better-business-makes-the-greater-good.

Mayer, C. 2018. "The Future of the Corporation: Towards Humane Business". Available at http://wlrk.com/docs/TheFutureoftheCorporationTowardsHumaneBusiness.pdf

Mayer, C. June 2020. "Shareholderism versus Stakeholderism – A Misconceived Contradiction." A Comment on "The Illusory Promise of Stakeholder Governance" by L. Bebchuk, and R. Tallarita. *European Corporate Governance Institute* (ECGI). Available at https://ecgi.global/content/working-papers

MIT Economics. 2020. "Labor in the Boardroom." Available at chrome-extension://oemmndcbldboiebfnladdacbdfmadadm/http://economics.mit.edu/files/17273

OECD. 2019. "OECD Insight: What Is Social Capital." Page 103. Available at https://oecd.org/insights/37966934.pdf

Organization of Economic Co-Operation And Development (OECD). 2018. "Human Capital – The Value of People." Available at https://oecd.org/insights/humancapital-thevalueofpeople.htm

Palladino, L., and K. Karlsson. 2018. "Towards "Accountable Capitalism": Remaking Corporate Law Through Stakeholder Governance." http://rooseveltinstitute.org/wp-content/uploads/2018/10/Towards-%E2%80%98Accountable-Capitalism%E2%80%99-issue-brief.pdf

Rezaee, Z., and N. Rezaee. 2020. "Stakeholder Governance Paradigm in Response to the COVID--19 Pandemic19 Pandemic." *Journal of Corporate Governance Research* 4, no. 1.

Rezaee, Z., and T. Fogarty. 2019. *Business Sustainability, Corporate Governance and Organizational Ethics.* John Wiley and Sons.

Sustainability Accounting Standards Board (SASB). November 2018. "Current Standards." Available at https://sasb.org/standards-overview/download-current-standards/

The Committee of Sponsoring Organizations of the Treadway Commission (COSO) and the World Business Council for Sustainable Development (WBCSD). 2018. "Guidance for applying Enterprise Risk Management (ERM) to Environmental, Social, And Governance (ESG)-Related Risks." https://docs.wbcsd.org/2018/10/COSO_WBCSD_ESGERM_Guidance.pdf

The World Economic Forum (WEF). 2020. "World Economic Forum Pledges to Stand By Stakeholders in the COVID-19 Era." Available at https://briefinggovernance.com/2020/04/world-economic-forum-pledges-to-stand-by-stakeholders-in-the-covid-19-era/

Warren, E. August 15, 2018. "Warren Introduces Accountable Capitalism Act." Available at https://warren.senate.gov/newsroom/press-releases/warren-introduces-accountable-capitalism-act

World Economic Forum (WEF). September 2020. "Measuring Stakeholder Capitalism Towards Common Metrics and Consistent Reporting of Sustainable Value Creation, White Paper." Available at https://wlrk.com/docs/WEF_IBC_Measuring_Stakeholder_Capitalism_Report_2020.pdf

About the Author

Zabihollah Rezaee (Zabi) is the Thompson-Hill Chair of Excellence, and Professor of Accountancy at the University of Memphis and has served a two-year term on the Standing Advisory Group (SAG) of the Public Company Accounting Oversight Board (PCAOB). He is currently serving on the Advisory Panel of the Hong Kong Financial Reporting Council. He received his BS degree from the Iranian Institute of Advanced Accounting, his MBA from Tarleton State University in Texas, and his PhD from the University of Mississippi. Dr. Rezaee holds 10 certifications, including Certified Public Accountant (CPA), Certified Fraud Examiner (CFE), Certified Management Accountant (CMA), Certified Internal Auditor (CIA), Certified Government Financial Manager (CGFM), Certified Sarbanes-Oxley Professional (CSOXP), Certified Corporate Governance Professional (CGOVP), Certified Governance Risk Compliance Professional (CGRCP), Chartered Global Management Accountant (CGMA), and Certified Risk Management Assurance (CRMA). He served as the 2012–2014 secretary of the Forensic Accounting Section (FAS) of the American Accounting Association (AAA), served on Auditing Standards Committee of the Auditing Section of the AAA, and is currently the editor of the *Journal of Forensic Accounting Research (JFAR)* one of the AAA journals. Dr. Rezaee was one of the finalists for the position of the Faculty Trustee at the University of Memphis in 2016 and the Ombudsperson position in 2017 and he is currently serving as the Chair of Budget and Finance Committee of the Faculty Senate at the University of Memphis.

Professor Rezaee has published over 240 articles and made more than 250 presentations, written 14 books and several book chapters, and has been invited as keynote speaker on business sustainability, corporate governance, and forensic accounting. Some of his books are as follows: *Financial Institutions, Valuations, Mergers, and Acquisitions: The Fair Value Approach*; *Financial Statement Fraud: Prevention and Detection*; *U.S. Master Auditing Guide*, 3rd edition; *Audit Committee Oversight Effectiveness*

Post-Sarbanes-Oxley Act; *Corporate Governance Post-Sarbanes-Oxley: Regulations, Requirements, and Integrated Processes*; and *Corporate Governance and Business Ethics and Financial Services Firms: Governance, Regulations, Valuations, Mergers, and Acquisitions.* His sustainability-related books are *Corporate Sustainability: Integrating Performance and Reporting*, published in November 2012, won the 2013 Axiom Gold Award in the category of Business Ethics, and *Business Sustainability: Performance, Compliance, Accountability, and Integrated Reporting*, published in October 2015 by Greenleaf Publishing. His most recent book on *Audit Committee Effectiveness* was published in three volumes by Business Expert Press in July 2016. His *Corporate Governance aftermath of the 2007–2009 Global Financial Crisis* in four volumes and *Forensic Accounting* in two volumes are published by Business Expert Press in July 2018 and March 2019, respectively. His new textbook on *Business Sustainability, Corporate Governance and Organizational Ethics* is published by Wiley in fall 2019. His most recent book entitled *Business Sustainability Factors of Performance, Risk and Disclosure* is published by Business Expert Press in March 2021. Several of these books are translated into other languages including Chinese, Persian, Korean, and Spanish.

Index

OTHER TITLES IN THE CORPORATE GOVERNANCE COLLECTION

John Wood, Editor

- *Business Sustainability and Profit-With-Purpose Focus* by Zabihollah Rezaee
- *A Primer on Corporate Governance* by Jose Luis Rivas
- *A Primer on Corporate Governance* by Andrea Melis and Alessandro Zattoni
- *A Primer on Corporate Governance* by Sibel Yamak and Bengi Ertuna
- *Managerial Forensics* by J. Mark Munoz and Diana Heeb Bivona
- *A Primer on Corporate Governance* by Jean Chen
- *Blind Spots, Biases, and Other Pathologies in the Boardroom* by Kenneth Merchant and Katharina Pick
- *A Director's Guide to Corporate Financial Reporting* by Kristen Fiolleau, Kris Hoang and Karim Jamal
- *A Primer on Corporate Governance, Second Edition* by Cornelis A. de Kluyver

Concise and Applied Business Books

The Collection listed above is one of 30 business subject collections that Business Expert Press has grown to make BEP a premiere publisher of print and digital books. Our concise and applied books are for...

- Professionals and Practitioners
- Faculty who adopt our books for courses
- Librarians who know that BEP's Digital Libraries are a unique way to offer students ebooks to download, not restricted with any digital rights management
- Executive Training Course Leaders
- Business Seminar Organizers

Business Expert Press books are for anyone who needs to dig deeper on business ideas, goals, and solutions to everyday problems. Whether one print book, one ebook, or buying a digital library of 110 ebooks, we remain the affordable and smart way to be business smart. For more information, please visit www.businessexpertpress.com, or contact sales@businessexpertpress.com.

Printed in Great Britain
by Amazon

32929495R00046